Making Friends in a New City:
A Guide to Thriving and Building Meaningful Connections

Introduction

This is a challenge faced by anyone moving to a new city. You relocate because you've found a new job, or you move for your education or studies. Your surroundings are entirely new, and you don't know anyone. Making friends, especially after turning 30, can be difficult for many people. You might meet colleagues at work, but finding friends with whom you can build deeper relationships is often more challenging. If this sounds familiar to you, then this book is exactly what you need!

In this book, I want to quickly outline the most important points and strategies that will help you build new and deep friendships wherever you are. However, for you to succeed, it is also essential that you engage in some critical self-reflection.

A few years ago, I moved all by myself from my hometown to Munich, where I knew no one. Today, I have a bigger circle of friends than I've ever had in my life, and I did this at the age of 30. These friendships didn't take long to form, either. Within my first two weeks, I met people who are still some of my closest friends today. Initially, I wasn't aware that I had a key with me that made finding friends easier. I only discovered the existence of this key when I read books by Dale Carnegie and Jack Schafer. Essentially, neither I nor these authors invented the principles I am about to discuss. They are not fundamentally new ideas, but simply concepts that these authors put into writing. Nevertheless, it is important for you to call these ideas to mind, understand them, and apply them. For some people, this process happens intuitively, while others need to consciously practice and control their actions. The key is within each of us. If you haven't yet found it, I will make it clear for you in this book. By understanding this key, you will be able to carry it with you and captivate people wherever you go. Whether you're looking for friends, close acquaintances, or the love of your life, knowing this key will help you establish meaningful connections no matter where you live. Whether you live in Berlin, Munich, New York, London, Paris, or Dubai, this key will open doors for you anywhere.

Strategies to Avoid

Before I explain how I found my friends, how I developed my strategies, and how I became aware of the key to making connections, I want to talk about what you shouldn't do.

A few years ago, I was standing at Munich Central Station waiting for a friend. While I was waiting, a woman approached me and tried to engage me in conversation. I responded politely, but the conversation and the situation made me feel uncomfortable. Unfortunately, I couldn't just walk away, as I was waiting for my friend exactly at that spot. Telling her that I wasn't interested in a conversation didn't seem like an option either. After all, I thought she should have noticed that the conversation was going nowhere. However, she didn't realize it and just kept talking. She told me that she didn't have any friends and was currently looking for people to befriend. I appreciated her attempt to change her situation, but her approach completely overwhelmed me, and I found myself hoping that my friend would arrive within a few minutes and save me.

The woman kept talking about herself and how unfair it was that she didn't have any friends. She asked me if I was in a relationship, to which I replied, "Yes, and I'm waiting for my girlfriend." She then said that she was also in a relationship. I found this a bit odd in that context, because if you want to get to know someone platonically, this kind of information really shouldn't matter.

When my friend finally arrived and "rescued" me, the woman who had approached me looked very sad. She didn't understand what she had done wrong and couldn't grasp why nobody wanted to spend time with her. The simple answer to this is: friendships don't work like that!

You can't just wander around aimlessly and convince yourself that the first person you approach will become your new best friend. The way she approached me, as well as the dialogue itself, was inappropriate. You have to be able to interpret the signals from the other person correctly to avoid wasting both their time and your own.

In the following chapters, I will explain what you should pay attention to and how you can behave to turn strangers into friends. I will keep the chapters as concise as possible so that you can quickly put what you've learned into practice after reading this book.

If you want further reading on this topic, I recommend the books "How to Win Friends and Influence People" by Dale Carnegie and "The Like Switch" by Jack Schafer.

Your Appearance

Your personal appearance is the first step in gaining others' sympathy. It may sound a bit trivial, but it bears repeating. A well-groomed appearance and neat clothing are crucial for the first impression, which determines whether people find us likable or unlikable. Dress in a way that suits your style and conveys that you are well-kept. Your clothing should fit the occasion: if you're in the city, wear a neat city outfit, and if you're doing sports, wear appropriate sportswear.

All of this is important for making a positive first impression. What's especially interesting about occasion-appropriate clothing is that you should avoid standing out negatively. By this, I mean that, for example, if you're at a music festival, wearing T-shirts of your favorite band can make you appear more likable to other fans, making it easier to strike up conversations. We will explore this point later when we discuss belonging and finding "common ground."

For a positive first impression, it's also important that you feel comfortable in your own skin. This is something you can achieve through your clothing and personal style. What you wear is actually secondary as long as your outfit makes you feel good. When you feel comfortable, you project confidence. The people you come into contact with will notice this and automatically be drawn to you.

Your confidence is another aspect that is crucial for a first impression. Your personal clothing style is just a small part of what can boost your confidence and self-assurance. In fact, you can also train your confidence, which will lead to even better results in your quest for new friends.

Your Body Signals

We humans can perceive body language both consciously and unconsciously. This involves much more than simply interpreting facial expressions. Our entire body communicates: our hands, feet, legs, and body posture are just as important as our facial expressions. We constantly send signals about how we feel. These signals can be influenced to some extent, but only for a limited period of time. Therefore, you should master your body language when approaching other people. Additionally, you should be able to recognize and correctly read the body language of others.

When you want to approach someone, make sure that the person is also sending open body signals. In principle, it is possible to approach people with negative signals and still succeed, but statistically speaking, it will be more difficult. If you do approach someone (regardless of whether they are sending positive or negative signals), you must pay attention to their body language during the conversation and interpret it correctly. If the person isn't asking you questions, seems defensive, and you are the only one keeping the conversation going, your efforts are unlikely to be successful. Therefore, it is important to continuously observe body language, adjust your own, and draw conclusions from it.

Practicing body language and understanding its signals is an important step in understanding how friendships and human communication work. The best way to practice body language is to observe other people and think about the relationship they might have with each other. Sit in a café, for example, and observe the people passing by. Even if they are walking alone, they are still sending signals. After all, one cannot not communicate. Let's go over the most important aspects of body language so you can properly observe and apply them for yourself.

Eye contact is a body language signal that is crucial for both initiating conversations and having a successful discussion. If you want to approach someone, start by establishing eye contact with that person. If they look at you and continue to send positive signals, you have a good chance that approaching them will be successful. During a conversation, eye contact says a lot about your relationship with the other person. If you and your conversation partner frequently maintain eye contact, it is a good sign of mutual sympathy. However, if the other person avoids your gaze and breaks eye contact, it can be taken as a negative sign. This does not mean, however, that you or the person you are talking to need to stare at each other constantly. On the contrary, staring for too long can come across as creepy and does not contribute to a comfortable atmosphere. Therefore, you should occasionally shift your focus to then reestablish eye contact again.

An open body posture is another signal you should pay attention to. It indicates both the success of the initial approach and interest in the ongoing conversation. One particularly important aspect is arm posture. If their arms are open and not crossed, it is a positive sign. If the arms are crossed, it can be interpreted as rejection. The direction the torso is turned is another indicator. If the person's torso is facing you, it can be interpreted as interest. Even the direction of the person's feet can give you clues about whether they are interested in the conversation. You're on the safe side if the person's feet are pointing toward you.

Whether people are actively listening can also be shown through their body language. If they are interested in the conversation, they lean in towards you, come closer, and nod during the conversation. Additionally, small verbal cues like "yes" and "I understand" are also signs of active listening.

People also show signals of personal closeness when they move closer to you and seek proximity in general. For example, they might pull their chair closer or turn their body towards you. The tilting of the head is particularly noticeable. If someone is listening to you and slightly tilts their head while maintaining eye contact, it expresses that they trust you. This gesture is especially common when dating. Evolutionarily, it is also quite interesting, as it shows openness and trust. When someone tilts their head, the carotid artery becomes slightly exposed — a vital area that people typically protect. When someone exposes this to you, it is a significant gesture of trust.

One signal you can use to check if someone is interested in a conversation with you is the quick raising and lowering of your eyebrows. If you make eye contact with a person and raise and lower your eyebrows within a few seconds, the other person will recognize this as a friendly signal. It is important, however, to make the raising of your eyebrows subtle. Holding it for just a millisecond too long can come off as creepy and produce the opposite effect.

The Law of Belonging

When you want to start a conversation with someone, it is easiest if you show empathy and use a shared commonality. The best way to do this is when you're at the same event. If you meet someone at a concert, you can be sure that you at least have one thing in common: you both like the same music. You can build on this common ground. If you are on a train heading to a marathon and see another person wearing running gear, it is very likely that they are participating in the same event. This provides a good opportunity to use that commonality to start a conversation. The person you approach may find you likable because you clearly share similar interests. This phenomenon can also be observed in political contexts. At party conventions or demonstrations, you'll find people who share the same political views. There is a common belief that you shouldn't talk about politics, money, or religion when getting to know someone, but if it is such an obvious attribute, you can still use it.

The "Law of Belonging," as I like to call it, does not only apply to events where shared interests are assumed. If you see someone in public wearing a jersey of your favorite sports team, it's reasonable to assume that they are also a fan of that team. You can use their jersey as an icebreaker for a conversation. Of course, it's easiest if you both happen to be wearing a jersey in public.

A conversation starts best with an empathetic approach. Base your approach on something you notice about the other person and try to put yourself in their position. Let's use the jersey example. An opening line might be:
"I see you're also a fan of Bayern Munich. How long have you been a fan?"

This type of approach isn't limited to external characteristics like clothing. If, for instance, you want to approach someone who is on their way home and probably had a stressful day at work, you can structure your approach similarly.

"You look like you've had a stressful day too." – this could also serve as an icebreaker for a conversation.

However, be mindful of the signals we discussed earlier. When approaching someone directly, the other person should already be giving appropriate signals. If you notice negative signals after you start the conversation, you can choose to end it as well.

Personal Space

Everyone has their personal space. This also applies to physical proximity. If you get too close to someone without their permission, they will reclaim their personal space. This means that they will move away from you and take a step in the opposite direction. You should always observe and respect this personal space. If you approach someone and step directly into their comfort zone, they will perceive it as an invasion of their privacy. This, in turn, reflects poorly on you, especially when you are just getting to know someone.

The size of the personal space a person needs can vary. It can be a matter of several meters, and it is particularly important to respect it when you're meeting someone for the first time. If you notice that someone feels uncomfortable after you approach them, you can take a step back to show that you respect their comfort zone.

There are situations when we allow other people to come closer. For instance, in a crowded train, we accept others being close to us because it makes sense — after all, they have limited space to move. However, if someone comes too close to us in an otherwise empty train, we perceive it as unsettling and it makes us feel uncomfortable.

When getting to know people, it's important to ensure that the person of interest feels comfortable. This sense of comfort should come from you, and your counterpart should associate this positive feeling with you. If you invade their personal space right away, they will no longer feel comfortable, which leaves a negative impression on your first meeting.

Once you get to know someone better, they will gradually allow you to come closer. Their comfort zone will adjust to accommodate you. They will give you permission to get closer. When this happens, it's a good sign and the first step toward building a lasting friendly relationship.

Use Human Catalysts

One of the reasons why some people find it easier to make new friends in a new environment than others is that they meet the right "human catalysts" at the right time. In chemistry, a catalyst is a substance that facilitates a reaction between two materials without itself being changed. There is something similar when it comes to friendships. A human catalyst is a person you meet who introduces you to others and speaks positively about you.

In the classic sense, it could be a bartender who knows everyone at the pub and introduces you to their customers. These people are the ones who break the ice for you, so you have to do less groundwork. It is important that you always leave a good impression in these kinds of connector relationships. This is because of what is known as the "primacy effect."

The primacy effect is a psychological phenomenon that deals with the initial biases that determine your image. Specifically, it means that the information the catalyst conveys about you shapes the preconceptions others have when they meet you. If the catalyst, for example, says that you are a friendly person, their friends are likely to perceive you as friendly—even if they meet you on a bad day. The primacy effect essentially precedes the classic first impression. This can work to your advantage, but also to your disadvantage. After all, your influence on what is said about you is limited. It is in the hands of others to determine what they say about you. If someone speaks poorly about you, the perception of others will be negatively influenced automatically.

The only way to fight against this is to avoid making a bad impression altogether. However, this is not always easy, especially when a reputation precedes you due to someone else's words. Be kind and courteous to every new person you meet. Ensure that even in a heated discussion, the other person always "saves face." If you do this, there will be no reason for others to tarnish your reputation in advance. However, there is no absolute guarantee.

The Law of Human Selfishness

People are selfish. Without exception! – What sounds harsh at first is a fact that cannot be denied. Even a person who has made it their life's mission to help others is selfish. Their goal might be the recognition they receive from the group they help or from another group. Their goal could also be the sense of superiority they feel from being helpful. With this in mind, you will begin to see conversations with others on a different level.

When you approach someone you want to befriend, your personal desire is to find a friend who makes you feel comfortable. Your counterpart has the exact same thought process. It makes no sense to try to be friends with someone whose company you don't enjoy. This is the root of a toxic relationship. Many people mistakenly hold on to such relationships, but that too is a selfish trait. People who hold on to toxic relationships often want to avoid pain on another level. They don't want to have an argument and feel bad for a brief moment. Instead, they just accept the toxic relationship.

Now let's get to how you can use the "Law of Human Selfishness" to make friends. Essentially, this law works similarly to marketing and sales. A potential friend has to recognize the value in you. While you're communicating with them, they are asking themselves: "What am I getting out of this conversation?" Even though they won't explicitly ask this question, you still have to answer it for them.

People like those who make them feel comfortable. You can make people feel comfortable around you by giving them what they want: attention. Every person is the main character of their own story. That is why people like to talk about themselves. They also enjoy hearing positive things about themselves. This gives you two opportunities to make new friends.

The first opportunity is to learn how to actively listen. We often tend not to listen properly to our conversation partner and instead start preparing our responses in our heads. If you catch yourself doing this, stop your train of thought and refocus on the words being said to you. Often, it's a simple keyword that causes us to drift off mentally. When you notice this happening, you need to re-center yourself and focus again on the conversation. An active listener will say very little besides occasional interjections like "I see" or "yes." Show your agreement through active nodding at a moderate level. Also, make sure you send positive body signals. This includes leaning forward, maintaining engaged but not staring eye contact, and occasionally tilting your head.

The second opportunity is to talk about your counterpart with them. Give compliments and, whenever the opportunity arises, ask follow-up questions about what they have shared with you during the conversation. This shows the person of interest that you were listening. People appreciate this.

Recognition

We have already emphasized in the previous chapter that recognition can help when getting to know new friends. Here, I want to focus specifically on the fact that you will attract people into your life if you treat them with respect and recognition. Everyone is the protagonist of their own movie, and they want to feel that way. We all crave recognition, and we appreciate those who give it to us. You can express this recognition in various ways.

The simplest way is direct praise. You can praise someone for a variety of things, even rather superficial ones, and in doing so, show your recognition. What's important is that the praise is sincere and communicated convincingly. You can make your praise more credible by adding a reason to it. This makes it harder for your words to be dismissed as insincere. Additionally, providing a reason extends the praise, which will further please the other person. This reason can be based on small details or be a compliment on someone's improvement at work.

You can also communicate your praise about a person to other people. On the one hand, this casts a positive light on you, because speaking well of others is generally appreciated, especially if people can assume you will also speak well of them when they aren't around. If the person in question is present when you do this, it can boost their self-esteem, which will further strengthen your personal relationship with them.

Consistency in showing recognition also contributes to the strength of your bond. So make sure you regularly show recognition to your friends.

Personal Openness

One of my best friends once told me, "When I first met you, I knew right away that you would be a good friend." This statement deeply touched me, as I still appreciate and admire my friend to this day. He is one of those people who have a special sense of understanding others and can accurately assess situations. What intrigued me most about this statement was what specific trait led him to that conclusion. His response was quite clear: "You are one of the most honest people on the planet. When you started to speak so candidly about your love life, I knew everything I needed to know."

It was only a few days later that I realized exactly what he meant and that there could be a fundamental principle behind it. When we open up to others and give them a glimpse into our private lives, we can connect with them much more quickly. It's a kind of give-and-take. I share personal information about myself with you, and in return, I get some from you. This exchange of information increases your familiarity, as you get to know each other better.

It is important, however, that while you should share some personal details, you should not share so much that you make yourself vulnerable. This is especially true when you are just getting to know someone. What specific information you choose to share depends on what wouldn't be harmful to you if that information were spread to strangers. This caution applies particularly during the first meeting. After all, you don't know the person yet, and you don't know if they might be a narcissist who could exploit that information. The information you share should not make you vulnerable but should still be personal enough that you wouldn't just share it with anyone.

The kind of information you share usually emerges naturally from the conversation. Whenever someone asks for your opinion, you can link your response with personal information. This technique is most effective when you are having a one-on-one conversation with another person. In that scenario, the sense of intimacy is stronger, and your counterpart will understand that you are placing your trust specifically in them and not in a general group. This, in turn, strengthens the personal bond between you and also gives the person of interest the opportunity to share their own information with you without hesitation. In this way, you get to know people even better.

The Law of Names

There is a sound that every person loves to hear: their own name. This ties in with what we've already discussed — that people see themselves as the main character of their own story and crave recognition. When you address someone by their name, it shows that you value them and that their name is important to you.

Make sure to remember the other person's name right after the introduction. If you don't catch it the first time, ask again briefly and then repeat it. It's even better if you repeat the person's name immediately after they introduce themselves and add something like, "It's nice to meet you." By repeating and saying the name out loud, it becomes easier for you to remember it.

During the conversation and while getting to know them, you should also use your conversation partner's name more often. This will make people pay more attention to you, and it's like music to their ears.

Know-It-Alls Without Friends

No one likes a know-it-all. There's a reason for this: when people correct others and constantly add their two cents, they make others feel inferior or inadequate. The know-it-all is trying to elevate their own status, but in doing so, they lose the opportunity to make new friends. But why is that?

As we have learned, every person is a selfish being who sees themselves as the main character of their own story. People want to maintain that main character status, so they are always mindful of their position. This status must not be attacked, and if it is, they form a negative impression of the attacker. The person who corrects others is not doing so to genuinely help expand someone else's perspective — they are doing it because it makes them feel superior. It's so obvious that most people immediately turn away from a know-it-all, and they end up standing alone in no time.

If you want to make friends, you need to be aware of this fact. This also applies to conversations with people who are already your friends. Everyone feels attacked when they are corrected.

But what do you do if, during a conversation, you realize that your conversation partner is actually wrong? The classic opening line that know-it-alls use is the well-known "Yes, but..." This phrase signals two things: that a know-it-all and corrective opinion is about to follow, and that you obviously weren't really listening. After all, if you had been listening, you wouldn't need to agree and then immediately take back your agreement. Instead, use the combination "Yes, and..." This shows that you're not correcting but rather expanding on the statement. In everyday life, making this shift isn't always easy, but it helps to observe both yourself and others in shared discussions.

Made in United States
Cleveland, OH
23 December 2024

12607207R00017